I0421614

Leave the Job Behind:

Easy Ways to Profit in Today's Digital Economy

Amy Harrop

Leave the Job Behind:
Easy Ways to Profit in Today's Digital Economy
by **Amy Harrop**

Printed in the United States of America

Published by **Arcana Publishing**
Copyright © 2015 **Amy Harrop**

Disclaimer

This book contains business strategies, marketing methods and other business advice that, regardless of my own results and experience, may not produce the same results (or any results) for you. I make absolutely no guarantee, expressed or implied that by following the advice below you will make any money or improve current profits, as there are several factors and variables that come into play regarding any given business.

Primarily, results will depend on the nature of the product or business model, the conditions of the marketplace, the experience of the individual, and situations and elements that are beyond your control.

As with any business endeavor, you assume all risk related to investment and money based on your own discretion and at your own potential expense.

Liability Disclaimer

By reading this book, you assume all risks associated with using the advice given below, with a full understanding that you, solely, are responsible for anything that may occur as a result of putting this information into action in any way, and regardless of your interpretation of the advice.

You further agree that our company cannot be held responsible in any way for the success or failure of your business as a result of the information presented in this book. It is your responsibility to conduct your own due diligence regarding the safe and successful operation of your business if you intend to apply any of our information in any way to your business operations.

Terms of Use

You are given a non-transferable, "personal use" license to this book. You cannot distribute it or share it with other individuals.

Also, there are no resale rights or private label rights granted when purchasing this book. In other words, it's for your own personal use only.

Table of Contents

Leave the Job Behind

Introduction

1

Leave the Job Behind

Welcome to: Leave The Job Behind: Easy Ways to Profit In Today's Digital Economy. I'm excited and honored that you have picked up this book. There is a lot of noise, misinformation and hype around making money outside the confines of a traditional job. I'm here to clear the air and deliver no-BS methods to successfully participate in the digital economy and make money.

The exciting thing about today's opportunities is that you don't have to go to business school, or even grow a big business to step outside the limiting confines of a 'job'. It is incredibly easy to provide goods, services, and value to others, and to get paid for it.

Who This Is For

Are you unsatisfied and frustrated with your current financial circumstances?

Are you bored or unfulfilled with your job, or simply not able to move forward and make the type of money you'd like to?

Leave the Job Behind

Do you get the nagging feeling that you shouldn't be working as hard as you do for such a small return?

It's time to expand out of the traditional confines of a job, where you are paid an hourly or salary wage in exchange for labor. There are so many ways to make more money, and have more time and more freedom. But only for those who can move forward.

Revealed

In: Leave The Job Behind I'm going to share:

- My personal journey to a full-time income without a job
- Why now is the best time to make the leap
- How to get started quickly—what you need and what you don't need
- The best methods for profiting and the tools and training to get started quickly
- Invaluable advice that I learned the hard way so you don't have to

Let's get started!

My Journey from Job to Online
Income

Leave the Job Behind

I've had many jobs over the years, and have truly enjoyed only a few of them. I wasn't someone like Richard Branson, born with a natural bent toward being an entrepreneur, but I did arrive at that point, after many years of feeling, Is that all there is?

That isn't to say that I didn't do a good well at my various jobs. In fact, I was consistently given good performance evaluations and often given raises or promotions. But I always felt like I was using a very small part of my talents and skills, and that at the end of the day they were benefiting someone else. It took me a while, but I eventually knew that working for myself was really the only way forward for me.

Like many, I started working part time when I was a teenager. I started off babysitting, and worked in a dentist's office for a summer filing, which was my first real job. I worked in retail at a Fred Meyer store, and spent a summer working for a snack and ice cream shop in the mall. The best part about these jobs was the feeling of camaraderie with the other coworkers, many of who were around my age or a few years older. In the

Leave the Job Behind

Summer months, we'd all get together afterwards often and party and have fun. I lived in Fairbanks, Alaska, and in the summer the sun never stops shining.

Over the years, I've done many different types of work. I've done a lot of office work, received a B.A. in film production, and I worked in the film industry for a period of time, which was interesting, but held too much fakery for my taste. I grew up in a lower income family in Alaska; at heart, I just really didn't fit in with the fakeness of Los Angeles.

I also taught adults English and transitioned into being a high school English teacher for three years. This was rewarding in some aspects, but the pay was so low with the amount of work that needed to be done, especially reading and correcting essays. I looked around at many of the other teachers and they had a true love for the kids. I liked kids, but that wasn't where my vocation lay. However, teaching English helped me hone my own writing skills.

One of the things—other than being an English teacher, which also strengthened my writing and

Leave the Job Behind

presentation skills—and that really helped me move into wanting to work for myself was doing sales. I had several sales jobs, primarily phone sales. My last one, which helped propel me into my first true entrepreneurial success, was as an insurance agent and taking inbound calls. I enjoyed sales, and I was very good at it.

Believe me, I was not a hard-sell salesperson; as a woman, I had a relatively soft, inviting voice, and I found that it worked very well over the phone. I might've stayed with the insurance company longer if it wasn't for the strenuous commute, and draconian measures there. You had to read from a script, they recorded everything, and they had very little flexibility in terms of hours. This was my last 'job'.

The Need for Freedom

Over the years, I developed a sense of freedom from moving. I moved from Alaska to San Francisco to Los Angeles and achieved a sense of independence. My family was far away. I had no children, and still don't. I met my husband when I was a teacher, which was the last job I had before

Leave the Job Behind

I took the insurance job. He was originally from England, and also on his own over here in the states. He owned his own business, and supported me in my explorations of alternative forms of income. In fact, today we work at home and work in our own separate businesses.

My point with all this is that it is never too late to start. I was in my early 30s, at the insurance job, and got into purchasing books and selling them online, primarily on Amazon. At the time, there were many treasures to be found at thrift stores, estate sales, library sales, etc. I've always loved books, always loved reading, and always loved browsing and finding treasures. With this, I was getting paid to do something I enjoy. It was so exciting to pick up a book for $.50 or a dollar, and then turn around and sell it online for $25 or more.

The Southern California area was also a great place to find books. It was easy to find lots of fantastic books with the proliferation of libraries, colleges, and upscale neighborhoods. In fact, because so many of the people who live there work in the entertainment industry, you could often find signed books by celebrities, which was even more rewarding.

After about six months of doing this part time, I decided to take the leap and walk away from my insurance job. This meant leaving a set salary, plus a commission, plus healthcare. And my husband was self-employed at the time as well. He owned a sign business. I became successful as an online seller, but there was also a big learning period. I had to learn how set up a business. Today there are a lot more easy online solutions to use to handle the business setup.

Although, over time, I eased out of selling books online, and moved to my greater love of writing and publishing, I will always have fond memories of that first real working-for-myself moment.

Making the Leap

Once I made the leap, I was able to move into other ways of allowing an income that didn't have to do with selling physical books. Instead, I got excited about the new digital publishing movement and the release of Amazon's Kindle e-book reader. I started writing and publishing e-books, and also moved into teaching, training, and helping others do the same.

Once I was able to shift my mentality from being an employee to someone who had more control over their income, it was very easy to continue on to the next endeavor. One of the things that helped me do that was having a variety of sales type jobs where part of my earnings was commission- based. There's something very freeing about knowing you are responsible for bringing in your income.

You Don't Need To Be a 'Business Person'

To make this shift, you don't have to be a salesperson or a business person. There are so many opportunities today to make your own income without having to work full time for a company. And that doesn't mean having to start up a big business with the business plan and tons of employees. That's what the focus of this book is; it's to help people like yourself break away from the perception that you're either an employee or a business owner. You can enjoy freedom and flexibility and income by doing work on your own terms.

And, yes, you will have to get some of the trappings of having a business, such as a business bank account, and a structure that allows you to operate as a business. But that is so easy to do today, and there it is, so much online help and easy ways you can set this up.

What you don't need to do

What you don't need to do is:

• Borrow money or get startup funding to launch a new business. Later in this book I'll be sharing some different business models with you, and most of these can be done part time, and bootstrapping, where you're able to reinvest your profits back into the business and grow it without borrowing money or getting startup funds.

• Spend a lot of money on equipment or training. There are many ways to bring in income without having to do advanced training, or buy a lot of equipment. However, many of these (but not all) are digitally oriented, so having a computer and reliable Internet connection is essential.

• Hire employees. You will probably need some freelance workers depending on what you are doing, and if you want to scale up. But, again, it is very easy today to hire people to provide and perform a wide variety of tasks for you. And you can do this quickly and easily without having to actually hire an employee.

• Take formal courses, or go to business school. There is no need to get involved in fancy business speak or job titles. In fact, this sort of MBA-style culture is often what holds a lot of people back from thinking that they can work for themselves. While lifetime learning is important, and you probably will be learning new skills as you get more involved in specific ways of creating income, you do not need to do any formal education and training.

What you should do:

Leave the Job Behind

•   Talk with an accountant who specializes in small or online businesses so you know how to set up your business.

•   Be prepared to set up separate structures for your business such as bank account, DBA, and online bookkeeping.

•   Set up payment options, so your business can get paid separately, ideally digitally. The most popular method of taking digital payments is currently PayPal, although there are other options such as Stripe, Square, and Google Wallet. I recommend getting set up with a PayPal business account. As a backup payment method, I also recommend Stripe, they process credit cards and they don't require a credit check or anything really.

- http://www.makeuseof.com/tag/set-paypal-account-business/
- http://smallbusiness.chron.com/set-up-business-paypal-account-2489.html
- http://orgspring.com/create-paypal-business-account/
- http://Stripe.com

Leave the Job Behind

The beauty of this is you can use your business setup for a wide variety of income producing methods—you don't have to limit yourself to one business. Because of this, I recommend that you choose a somewhat generic business name that could be applied to different types of businesses.

Basic Setup

So, here are the essentials you need to get started:

• A computer or access to a computer with a reliable Internet connection. In order to participate in many of these opportunities, which have become available because of today's digital economy, it's essential that you have a way to do work and present your work online. This doesn't mean you need to be a computer programmer or super computer savvy, but we want to go where the opportunities are and there are a lot of opportunities available in the online economy.

• A business identity, with the right structure for tax purposes. You may need to talk to an accountant and determine whether being an

Leave the Job Behind

independent contractor with a doing business as (DBA) name, or starting an LLC or corporation would be the best for you. You can do all of these things relatively low cost.

• A separate business bank account and a way to take payments online, preferably PayPal with a backup option, such as Stripe.

• Some type of bookkeeping or accounting software. There are now a lot of great options for online businesses and small businesses. I recommend a service like http://outright.com. They are geared toward online businesses, and make it very easy to manage everything. Unless you are already familiar with QuickBooks, I don't recommend a complicated program like that unless you have someone else handle your accounting.

These are the types of things you can be getting together while you start setting up. However, you don't want to wait too long, as the more you are in business the more you will need to have these elements in place.

Digital Economy

Leave the Job Behind

I've been talking a little bit about the concept of the digital economy. What is the digital economy?

According to Wikipedia:

"Digital Economy refers to an economy that is based on digital computing technologies. The digital economy is also sometimes called the Internet Economy, the New Economy, or Web Economy. Increasingly, the "digital economy" is intertwined with the traditional economy making a clear delineation harder."

The digital economy is based on the role that computers and other types of electronics have in our society today. We can now read content, watch videos, chat with people, and purchase things all online. Because this is such a new and rapid development, there are so many opportunities that are growing and changing rapidly. And, of course, opportunities that were available in the past are no longer easy or available.

But there is room for many people to make money and replace or supplement their income with the

Leave the Job Behind

digital economy. You do not need to resign yourself to being a wage slave, and working for somebody else, nor do you need to grow into a multimillion dollar corporation and hire tons of employees. In today's digital economy, you can have a thriving business on your terms. And that is what is exciting about this. This opportunity is for everybody, just look around and see the potential.

Leave the Job Behind

Profiting from the
Digital Economy

Leave the Job Behind

Getting Started

While you're getting your basic setup in place, it's time to start thinking about what you'd like to actually do. One of the benefits of profiting from the digital economy is that you are not locked into just doing one thing. That being said, you do want to make sure you are focused and give something enough time to grow. In this following section, I'm going to go over various skills and how you can apply them to create an income.

I suggest you focus on one or two areas based upon your own skill set, experience, and inclination. Once you have something up and running, you can always grow it or get involved as well. But, I really caution you not to start multiple things at once. This is one of the biggest causes of failure for people who are trying to create an income online. They don't stay focused, and they start giving their attention to lots of different things.

Tools and Training

Another thing to be aware of is that, once you start exploring online income possibilities, you'll see

Leave the Job Behind

that you'll encounter many opportunities to get additional training and tools. A lot of these can be very helpful, but, again, I would caution you against purchasing any type of additional training or tools at first. A lot of times, you can succeed with just bare-bones, and then you can scale up from there or reinvest your profits and get additional tools and training.

There is a lot you can learn and you do not want to be in the business of being a perpetual student. Make sure, before you invest in any type of training, that you have a specific plan to apply it to boost your income, don't just take training, or purchase training courses because you vaguely might need them in the future. That's a good way not only to waste money, but also suck up your time, and contribute to a lack of focus.

Learning Recommendations

If you decided you want to learn something specific, and you are finding it easily online, a good place to pick up additional skills, and also a good place to bring in additional money, is the site called Udemy.com They often run sales, and you

Leave the Job Behind

can pick up classes in a wide variety of areas, for free or as little as $10. If you want to pick up technical skills, Lynda.com has a huge library of courses, and you can access them all for a small monthly fee.

Leave the Job Behind

Skills and Profit

Leave the Job Behind

In this section, I'm going to go over different skills, and different ways you can use them to profit. Like anything economic, the digital economy relies on exchanging some type of goods or services for remuneration. That means we're not talking about get-rich-quick schemes here, or anything that promises that you can make money without doing much of anything. Those are suckers' games and, unfortunately, you'll find them in great abundance once you start poking around online. In this guide, I'll be referring to legitimate ways you can generate an income by exchanging goods and services for cash.

There is a lot more leverage, though, that you can use in the digital economy, as far as trading your time for income. The goal is to be making much more hourly that you could at a job, and also having fun in the process. That being said, it's important to keep in mind what you want your time to be worth and you will probably adjust that as you continue to bring in money.

There will probably also be a startup period where you're putting in the time and effort but the money isn't coming in. However, if you apply yourself

Leave the Job Behind

diligently, and follow my tips and strategies, you should be able to bring in income relatively quickly, in a matter of weeks rather than months or years. And once that starts happening, you need to be thinking about what your time is worth and how you can continue to be more efficient so you can increase what you are giving yourself as an hourly wage.

Digital Economy Profit Centers

Leave the Job Behind

In this part of this book, I'm going to be sharing the specifics of the digital economy profit centers. These are specific strategies, skills, and tasks you can do to generate both an immediate and, in some cases, a passive income. Also, there may be some crossover with some of these profit centers.

Services

Leave the Job Behind

Service is really an umbrella heading, where you can perform tasks that are digital economy profit centers as a service for others, such as:

- Individuals
- Individual businesses
- Companies that are middlemen. You do the work for them and then they pass it on to somebody else. Often, these are the easiest places to get started with, but you don't want to stay there for long because you will be limiting your profits. Their business model depends on paying you less, and charging more for the end result. However, if you really want to see if something is for you, this can be a great place to start.

What Can You Offer As A Service?

Many skills you learn for your own income can also be used for other people. You can also concurrently offer your services as well as use them for yourself. Here are a few different skills that are in demand and that people will pay for.

Leave the Job Behind

•   Writing. Writing articles, short reports, and books for others is one of the easiest and fastest ways to get started. In fact, there are many companies that will pay you for your writing services, and once you have some practice under your belt, you can then start working with clients directly. Here are some places that will pay you to write for them:

- http://iwriter.com
- http://needanarticle.com/index2/naa-writer/
- https://www.triond.com/
- https://www.textbroker.co.uk/

•   And here is some training for launching your own writing business, and taking advantage of other opportunities.

- http://editingandwritingservices.com/articles-by-judy-vorfeld/start-editing-writing-business/
- http://www.wikihow.com/Start-a-Home-Based-Writing-Business'
- http://www.wow-womenonwriting.com/48-FE6-HowToStartWritingBusiness.html

Leave the Job Behind

•   Design and graphic services. These are in ever-increasing demand, and can range from branding and image design to website design.

•   Social media services. Setting up and managing social media content can be time-consuming. You can offer this as a service.

•   Services for local and small businesses. These can cover a wide array of services such as video production, writing, social media marketing—basically, anything that will help this business make money with an online presence.

•   Arbitrage, or connecting people in need of services with people who provide services. With this model, you are the middleman and you are providing services for people who need them, but you are contracting out the actual services. For example, one of the largest freelancing sites now is http://Upwork.com . You could offer services there, and then fulfill them with lower-cost workers.

•   Localized virtual services. This is a term I sort of made up to refer to services, you can register for more you provide and real life services. The real life services are offered locally, and can be things like running errands, doing chores, things like that. Basically, you would be a virtual or personal assistant and people will call in and ask you to do different things. These services have become increasingly popular, as people are so busy now that they are looking to outsource things like making travel reservations, picking up dry cleaning, and so on. If you're interested, the popular sites that you can register for are:

- Task Rabbit - https://www.taskrabbit.com/become-a-tasker
- Fancy Hands - https://www.fancyhands.com/job/apply/

Writing

While overall online communication is moving more toward video, there is still a large need for written content. If you have average to above average writing skills, this is one of the fastest and easiest ways to get involved in the digital economy. There are innumerable ways to write and get cash, some of these will allow you to earn an income immediately, and some may take a little bit longer. This is probably my favorite way to make money, and it is also flexible and versatile.

What You Need

There are different types of writing you may be doing, and I'll be going into the different methods here. It is essential that you stay focused, are able to write relatively quickly, and have some type of workflow organization in place. Here are a few tips and strategies:

•   Write first, revise later. This one simple rule will make sure that you have productive writing time, and that you are able to create blocks of content. You can always go back and revise and edit later.
•   Speaking of editing later, if you feel you're getting bogged down with the editing, you can get decent quality editors at freelancing sites like Fiverr.com and Upwork.com. One of the things that's really great about the digital economy is being able to outsource or give other people tasks you can't or don't want to do yourself. If you

Leave the Job Behind

haven't checked out Fiverr you will want to as you can get a variety of tasks done starting at five dollars.

However, if you are starting from scratch and don't want to do this, be sure to set aside some time after you finish writing to edit it yourself. You can rely on spellchecking programs, and also there are some online tools like Grammerly.com that will read and analyze your work. I normally do most of my own editing if I'm writing primarily for the direct market, such as for information products. However, if I am writing something that might be resold for a client or has a wider market, such as a book, I usually just work with an editor. They always catch stuff I might miss, and doing that type of copy-editing is not super fun for me.

•   If your writing involves research, come up with a way to research quickly before you start writing, or have someone do research for you.

•   Mind mapping and/or outlining what you are going to cover before you write can make writing much faster and easier. I like to do either or both depending on the length and type of content.

Leave the Job Behind

You'll want to find what works best for you, but it does help you structure your ideas better, and it helps avoid that blank page syndrome, because then you have something to start with. Mind mapping tools and links

- http://lifehacker.com/five-best-mind-mapping-tools-476534555
- http://www.digitaltrends.com/computing/best-mind-mapping-tools/
- http://mashable.com/2013/09/25/mind-mapping-tools/

• Consider using dictation software. The best software on the market is Dragon NaturallySpeaking. In fact, I've used that software to write the bulk of this book. While dictating seems to work a little differently when you're writing rather than typing, it can help free up thoughts, and allow content to flow faster and easier. Just be aware that when you dictate content you definitely need to edit it and sometimes it requires more revision.

Leave the Job Behind

Writing Opportunities

Because content online relies so much on the written word, there are numerous opportunities to build an income selling your writing.

•   Writing services. With writing services, you are basically a contractor for hire and you are writing for others. You can go through many companies that offer articles, blog posts, and other types of writing for clients. You basically sign up, give them some samples, and get started. The pay is usually not that great at first, but as you work your way up, you'll start getting paid more and being more in demand—if your writing quality is solid. However, you probably won't make as much money as if you work directly for yourself. If this is something that appeals to you, you can easily set up a site and offer your services directly. Check out the writing resources in the services section.

•   Blogging. If you are writing on a blog, the idea will be to write in an interesting voice so you can build followers. You can blog on nearly any topic that people are interested in. Bloggers make money from several avenues. The most common are advertisements on their site, and recommending other companies' products or services, which is called affiliate marketing. You can also sell content to your followers and fans directly from your site. Here is some information on getting started as a blogger:

- https://www.examtime.com/blog/how-to-become-a-successful-blogger/
- http://www.quickanddirtytips.com/education/grammar/how-to-get-started-blogging
- http://www.socialmediaexaminer.com/getting-started-with-blogging/

•   Selling digital content. This is actually a very broad market. You can go through a service like Amazon, or the iBookstore, and sell your content in the form of e-books on their platforms. It will take you a few months to start getting paid, but this can be a great way to build up an income over time. Here are some self-publishing resources:

- http://www.writersdigest.com/editor-blogs/there-are-no-rules/general/the-best-101-on-self-publishing-resources

Leave the Job Behind

- http://www.go-publish-yourself.com/
- http://selfpublishingresources.com/

•   You can also sell digital content directly through your own sales page, this works really well with info products or training. You can do these products over pretty much anything that people have problems with or need a solution for, and there are platforms where you can put the product on there and have other people promote your product for you. There is a bit of a learning curve with this, but it can be very lucrative, and is one of my favorite ways to make an online income.

•   Fiction. Writing fiction is more popular than ever. People can now read fiction quickly and conveniently on their Kindle, their phone, and other reading devices. And other people cannot see what they are reading, so they are free to indulge. If you enjoy writing fictional stories, this can be an incredibly lucrative market to be involved in. Particularly with fiction, the more you write the more you make. And it really benefits you to do research and find the most popular genres. Currently they are romance, mystery, and fantasy/sci-fi. However, there is huge variation within all of these areas. You can self-publish, and, with some diligence and time, you can build up a following. Here are some fiction writing resources:

- http://www.heretocreate.com/2007/11/01/re sources-for-fiction-writing/
- http://www.fictionaddiction.net/
- http://www.fictionfactor.com/links.html

In conclusion, writing is one of my favorite ways to create an online income. You can even combine several types of writing so you can get paid directly for what you're doing, such as providing writing services, and also building up more of a long-term passive income, such as publishing e-books.

In addition, writing can also be parlayed into more extensive teaching or training programs. You can offer full-on courses, coaching, consulting, and other types of training. I'll be exploring these later in this book.

Leave the Job Behind

Ecommerce

E-commerce is one of the best ways to get started earning an online income. Many, many people have been able to successfully replace and even increase their former job income with e-commerce. In fact, this is where I first got started, and I still do some e-commerce today, even.

What is e-commerce? It is selling physical products online. If you've purchased something online from Amazon or eBay, or anywhere else, and had it delivered to your home, you have participated in e-commerce.

E-commerce is one of these things that, with new technology and tools, is easy for people to get started with. There are two basic ways you can get started with e-commerce. You can either sell products directly on sites designed for that purpose, or you can sell products from your own website. Many successful sellers do a combination of both.

Leave the Job Behind

Selling on Other's Sites

While eBay has been around for a long time, the biggest growth in e-commerce has really come from Amazon. Amazon's FBA program (Fulfillment by Amazon) allows sellers to ship their goods to Amazon's warehouses, located across the country and even in many other countries as well, and list them on the Amazon marketplace, which has seen exponential growth.

FBA sellers are also able to sell to Amazon's prime members as well. Prime members get free two day shipping along with other benefits. E-Commerce has become a multimillion dollar business, and there are now many sellers who sell on Amazon's FBA program. Amazon will also fulfill products to other sites as well so you can sell on eBay too, and other types of sites.

Putting your products on Amazon, and having them fulfill your products to their customers and then even branching out and also listing on eBay, is really the fastest and easiest way to get started in e-commerce.

You can learn more here:

- http://services.amazon.com/fulfillment-by-amazon/benefits.htm?ld=NSGoogleAS
- http://services.amazon.com/content/seller-resources-how-to-guides.htm

Selling On Your Own Site

Because of new technology and tools, it is now easy to get an e-commerce website set up. Services like http://Shopify.com allow you to set up a website that sells products quickly and easily. They provide the checkout where people can pay and then you receive the payment. This has made it extremely easy to get started in e-commerce. Of course, you still have to get traffic to your site, which is why I recommend selling on other sites like Amazon first and leveraging the huge amounts of traffic that they get. However, this is a great way to expand if you are already selling or if you have the ability to bring traffic to your site.

Leave the Job Behind

Getting Started

E-commerce relies on sourcing inventory, listing inventory, and fulfilling inventory. Those are the three main components in any type of e-commerce business.

Sourcing inventory

If you enjoy finding deals, you can source a wide variety of sellable inventory at places like first stores, yard sales, and estate sales. In fact, my e-commerce business was primarily used books. This is a lot of fun, but it can be difficult to grow into a sustainable business if you are the one out there looking for inventory all the time. Over time, you would want to expand and sell wholesale inventory, or build a team of people who can help you find inventory.

That being said, this is a great way to get started and see immediate results. In fact, you can even get started with stuff you probably have lying

43

around your house. You can sell used books on both Amazon and eBay, but if you have other types of used inventory, eBay is probably the best place to start as Amazon has a lot of listing restrictions.

Many people who are building a full-time income through Amazon FBA are sourcing new inventory. They are often getting it manufactured and selling it under their own name so they are not competing with other sellers, or they are bundling it with other types of products in creating their own unique product line. There are a ton of resources out there for being successful with e-commerce, many of them free. Here are some sources you can use to get started:

- http://www.entrepreneur.com/article/246223
- http://www.entrepreneur.com/article/248142

Listing inventory

There are many tools that help you list your inventory on Amazon, your website, or other types of e-commerce sites quickly and easily. One of the big keys to succeeding with e-commerce is

Leave the Job Behind

streamlining and automating. If you enjoy systems, productivity, and stats, e-commerce can be a great place to excel in. Here are some resources for listing inventory:

- http://www.inventorysource.com/videos-training-guides/
- http://blog.capterra.com/the-top-5-free-inventory-software-systems/

Fulfilling inventory

This is where Amazon FBA comes into play. They have an awesome infrastructure in place for getting your inventory to customers. They will even fulfill inventory that you have listed on other sites if you have their inventory storage and warehouse. A lot of times people will also supplement what they are doing on Amazon with their own e-commerce website, and then use another type of fulfillment company, which can sometimes be cheaper.

Leave the Job Behind

Videos

Leave the Job Behind

The future is here. Videos have become the primary source of content on the Internet and video is expected to continue to increase in popularity.

• Online video now accounts for 50 percent of all mobile traffic and up to 69 percentof traffic on certain networks. (Bytemobile Mobile Analytics Report)

• The average user spends 88% more time on a website with video. (Source: Mist Media)

• 52 percent of consumers say that watching product videos makes them more confident in online purchase decisions. (Invodo)

How can you turn videos into an income stream? There are a number of ways you can use videos to make money. Before I go into the specifics, I must explain that it is now easier than ever to make professional videos. There are a number of video creation software tools that have been released. Some of these newer ones have been designed specifically for marketers, they are incredibly easy to use and do not require a lot of tech savvy. Here are some of the tools that are now available:

List of tools

In addition, many of the videos do not require you to be on screen, or anything along those lines. For example, animated videos are now really popular, and it is easier than ever to create these types of videos with today's technology.

The fact is, videos get a lot of traffic and if you decide to focus on videos you have the ability to create multiple streams of income. Here are a few ways:

•   Provide videos for others. These can range from product reviews, information type videos, sales videos, explainer videos, and more. You can provide videos as a service on sites like fiver.com and Upwork.com

•   Promote products as an affiliate with videos. Affiliate marketing can be a great way to bring in additional money, and I will cover this in a later section. Videos can be an easy way to review

Leave the Job Behind

products and get traffic back to your affiliate link. Here are some videos that are very popular, and are doing just that:

- https://www.youtube.com/watch?v=ap2gHk A_YVw
- https://en.wikipedia.org/wiki/List_of_most_vi ewed_YouTube_videos
- http://www.wsj.com/video/browse/most-popular

•   Video ads. This is a little bit more difficult, but there are a number of people on YouTube i who have channels that have huge followings, and they make a very nice stream of income from the advertising that they have on their videos. Google owns YouTube, and coordinates a variety of advertising opportunities for YouTube videos. The thing is many of these people aren't doing anything super complicated or exciting with their videos, they just managed to build up a following.

If you're excited about the possibilities of videos, this is a really great niche to be in, because videos are so popular, and will continue to increase in popularity as a form of online content.

Advice and Expertise Sharing

Leave the Job Behind

Did you know that you can get paid, often by the minute, for your advice and expertise? The digital economy is now providing plenty of platforms where you can register as an expert, and have hours where you're available to take calls, chat messages, or answer emails from people who are seeking advice. This is something that would probably not be a full-time stream of income right out of the gate, but it's definitely something that could turn into a more substantial stream of income and you can parlay it into additional courses, products and services, which I'll discuss in the next section.

What Do You Know?

If nothing springs to mind, sit down and make a list of everything you have some knowledge or training on. It could be things like:

•   topics that you took on-the-job training for or class training for, such as:

- QuickBooks and accounting
- various computer skills
- specialized occupational training

Leave the Job Behind

- hobbies such as:

  - photography
  - sports
  - cooking

- academic subjects such as:

  - history
  - education

Chances are you know more than you think you do and you have knowledge in some areas that people would be willing to pay for. This is also a fun way to talk about what you already know and enjoy doing, and to boost your self-confidence to take your skills to the next level.

Here are some sites where you can register and as an expert and get paid:

- https://hourlynerd.com/
- https://www.createpool.com/
- http://www.ether.com/default.aspx
- http://www.experts123.com/

Leave the Job Behind

Online Courses

Leave the Job Behind

Creating and selling online courses is really just an extension of sharing your expertise with others, as discussed in the previous section. This is also related to creating and selling products, which I'll discuss later. One of the reasons I want to talk about online courses first is that there are many opportunities to take advantage of already built infrastructure for online courses, meaning that you will supply the content and upload it, and they will offer it or sell it on their site.

Most online courses are structured in a module format. You would break down the topic to be covered into sections. In addition, many online courses have a focus more on video with supplementary materials included. This does not mean that you need to be a video expert to create these online courses. There are a lot of affordable video tools out there, and in many cases you can create online courses simply from recording yourself talking over a slideshow.

One caution with these types of courses is not to make them too big, especially when creating your first one. You want to pick a small sub topic. For example, let's say you have some expertise in, or knowledge about, cake decorating. A good first course would not be an introduction to cake decorating, but something much smaller, perhaps like easy cake decorating for beginners.

The best way to devise an online course is to first create an outline of what you're going to cover and divide that into modules or sections. It makes sense, and for each module, or section, it would be a good idea to provide a combination of video and written training. You may also want to provide some quizzes or review types of content so people can apply and remember what they've learned.

Where to Sell your Online Courses

There are a number of places where you can sell your online courses. You simply upload your course content, meet their course standards, and they will handle hosting the course and the payments. Some of these sites will also provide visibility and marketing as well. If you are looking for a longer-term plan I would suggest using courses that are hosted by others as a way to get people to know, like and trust you, in addition to also bringing in income. At the end of the day, I always think it's best to have more control over how your content is sold and distributed. But this can be a great way to get started.

The largest online course site currently is http://Udemy.com . They have grown by leaps and bounds over the last three years, and are huge. You can make course sales there without having to do a lot of marketing yourself, but the way they sell most of the courses is by having ongoing sales, so your course may be listed for more than it sells regularly. Here's some info and links on getting started with Udemy:

- https://support.udemy.com/customer/portal/articles/1587467-getting-started-guidelines?b_id=3213
- https://support.udemy.com/customer/portal/articles/1885837-getting-started-how-do-i-create-my-udemy-course-

Udemy also offers a free course on their platform on how to create a course. I recommend you take that, because not only will you learn what they are looking for, you can also see how content is

Leave the Job Behind

delivered on their platform from a student's perspective. LINK

- https://www.youtube.com/watch?v=GfrsfGSEKZI
- https://www.udemy.com/official-udemy-instructor-course/
- http://www.blogsmartguide.com/beginners-guide-create-udemy.html

Udemy does not require exclusivity, and once you have your course content done you can then submit it to other places that will sell your course for you. Here is list of other places to sell your course:

- http://coursemania.com/top-5-places-to-sell-your-training-online/
- http://www.learningrevolution.net/sell-online-courses/
- http://robcubbon.com/udemy-alternatives-selling-video-courses-online/

Leave the Job Behind

Ideally, you would also upload and sell your course yourself, but that does require some infrastructure that also leads into the next section about selling your own products yourself.

Leave the Job Behind

Products

Leave the Job Behind

Selling products has, for me, been my best source of online income, and second has been e-commerce. I don't necessarily recommend selling your own products first, because there really are some technical considerations and infrastructure you have to have in place and there are many other places you can do similar types of work, such as creating content and selling without having to do all of the preparation.

But if you have decided to go down one of the paths of content creation, such as writing or creating content for others or creating courses, then creating your product is really the next step.

One of the other great things about creating a product is that you have a basis to repurpose it then. You can then adapt it into a book or expand it into an online course.

There are four main things you need:

- A product
- A way to sell the product (sales page, etc.)
- An audience
- Product payment and delivery

Leave the Job Behind

There are a number of tools out there now that handle product payment and delivery for you. In addition, these tools often make it easier to have affiliates sign up, and sell your product automatically too. Here are some of the tools and services that you can use:

- http://www.pixel77.com/top-15-powerful-platforms-selling-digital-products/
- http://ecommerce-platforms.com/ecommerce-selling-advice/top-10-best-ways-sell-digital-goods-online

Product

The type of product that you create can be very similar to what you might create for an online course, such as a series of videos or video training. However, you can also do something that is more written-text heavy and create an e-book as well, or a combination of different formats. Similar to creating your first online course, your first product should not be too complicated and limited to one subtopic. Don't worry if you don't cover everything.

Leave the Job Behind

And remember, most people buy products because they want solutions. Keep your product focused on one problem, one solution.

Sales Page

For your first product, you can keep your sales page pretty basic. Go look at what other people are doing, who have similar types of products out there. I would suggest writing the actual text yourself, and modeling it on what other people are doing. However, if it's something you're getting stuck on, you can always outsource it to somebody else. You can format it into a plain HTML document, or many of the new WordPress style sites that have built-in sales page templates.

An Audience

The best way to sell digital products is through email. That means you have a list of subscribers and you send them an email about your product, or you get affiliates to send emails to their subscribers and they will get a percentage of the sales. However, you may not have any subscribers and you may not know any affiliates.

Leave the Job Behind

The best thing to do is to build up a list of subscribers by giving them free content related to your product in exchange for their email. The fastest and easiest way to do this is through paid advertising but you really need to be careful as you can end up spending a lot of money. You can also use free methods as well.

Paid Advertising

There are a number of paid advertising methods out there. I am not a paid advertising expert, but here are a few different platforms that I have used to successfully get subscribers. While you can directly advertise a product, oftentimes it is better to advertise a subtype of content and then have people get onto your list where you can keep in touch with them and sell them your products.

Here are some solid paid advertising sources:

Facebook Ads

- https://www.facebook.com/business/products/ads

- http://sproutsocial.com/insights/facebook-advertising-guide/
- http://digitalmarketingphilippines.com/the-ultimate-guide-on-facebook-paid-advertising-2014-edition/

Bing Ads

- http://advertise.bingads.microsoft.com/en-us/home
- http://www.wordstream.com/blog/ws/2015/02/25/bings-ads-vs-google-adwords
- http://www.koozai.com/blog/pay-per-click-ppc/bing-pay-per-click-ppc/advertise-on-bing/

Rent-A-list

- http://www.rent-a-list.com/

Free Methods

Free methods can also work, but they tend to take longer and require more elbow grease. I think the best free methods rely on content marketing. So, if you've already created content for a product you

Leave the Job Behind

can take smaller pieces of that content and rewrite or rework it. You can then use that content for:

- Blog posts
- PDFS
- Slideshows
- Videos
- Social media

And you will share them for free. This method requires using keywords that people would normally use to search for your product in your title and your description. You would then create your content in the following formats, and then post it to different places. Here are some links where you can post different types of content: slideshow, pdf, and video sharing platform links.

- http://www.entrepreneur.com/article/246369
- https://blog.bufferapp.com/content-distribution-tools
- http://www.bitrebels.com/social/content-posting-flowchart-guide/
- http://coschedule.com/blog/repurpose-your-content/

Affiliate Marketing

Affiliate marketing and product creation often go hand in hand. They are really complementary digital economy models, and affiliate marketing is another favorite income stream of mine as well. Being an affiliate means you recommend a third party's products or services, and if people buy or get the product or service through your link, you get a cut of the profits. This can be a competitive market, but people are always looking for high-quality recommendations.

This is also easier to do if people already know, like or trust you, which is why I have put it more toward the end of this section, because you really want to build a relationship with people first for best results. In addition, there are some legal requirements for affiliate marketing, such as you must disclose that you are going to be compensated somewhere near or in your content.

You can make product recommendations as an affiliate in a variety of ways. The two most popular and effective are through a blog, and through email marketing. In fact, you can combine both of these for powerful results.

With the blog, you would have blog posts that have content and product recommendations. People would find your blog through search engines, social media and other types of promotion, and paid traffic promotion. In addition, you can also build an email list using similar methods so that you could email people and provide quality content, and also product recommendations.

In addition to building an email list through a variety of traffic methods, you can also have people visit your blog and then have the option to get on your email list. This works best with a pop-up over your blog where people can sign up.

Setting up and running a blog is not incredibly difficult, but it does require some technical skills, or the ability to have somebody set it up and do it for you. The same goes for email marketing. But, if you are going to the trouble and time and energy of building an audience, recommending products and services to them is a great way to easily make an additional income. The key is to continue to offer content of value to them and make sure your recommendations also have value. You should try to review the products you are recommending as much as possible and if you are not able to recommend a product (perhaps being unable to see it yourself) you should make sure to look up product reviews.

Here are some resources on getting started with affiliate marketing:

- http://www.seanogle.com/entrepreneurship/how-to-start-affiliate-marketing
- http://www.tylercruz.com/how-to-get-started-in-affiliate-marketing-with-no-money/
- http://www.humanproofdesigns.com/affiliate-marketing-beginners/
- http://www.wikihow.com/Start-an-Affiliate-Marketing-Business

Leave the Job Behind

Conclusion

Leave the Job Behind

I'm confident that you have the skills, interest, and ability to get started with at least one of these digital profit centers. Once you get started, you can learn and grow over time and implement more. Remember, you don't need to have a business degree or work 90 hours a week to profit in today's digital economy.

Leave the Job Behind

More

Leave the Job Behind

Want more action steps to get started? Check out my free training on the publishing passive income stream here:

http://amyharrop.com/pages/easykindlepubsystem/
You can also follow me on my blog at
http://AmyHarrop.com

Enjoyed this book? Leave a review and spread the word!